people:

Unfinished Poems

RUTH IRWIN

RENARD PRESS

RENARD PRESS LTD

124 City Road
London EC1V 2NX
United Kingdom
info@renardpress.com
020 8050 2928

www.renardpress.com

'Central Line Sonnet' first published as 'London Sonnet' in *Earth-Quiet: Poems from Tower Poetry 2012* by Tower Poetry, Oxford in 2012
'Dig', 'Capital Story' (originally titled 'July') and 'On Those Cold December Evenings' first published in *Goldfish 2015* by Goldsmiths, University of London, in 2015
'The Greenfinch in the Garden' first published in *Red on Bone* by Poems Please Me in 2015
People: Unfinished Poems first published by Renard Press Ltd in 2023

Text and illustrations © Ruth Irwin, 2023

Printed in the United Kingdom by Severn

ISBN: 978-1-913724-99-3

9 8 7 6 5 4 3 2 1

Contents

people:

unfinished poems

DEDICATIONS:

For my parents,
      Stephen and Deborah,
who gave me my first words.

For my editor, Will,
  who gave me the space
  to make this book.

And for my partner,
      Pradyumna,
who gave me his heart.

THANK YOU.

              − love, Ruth.

chapter 1

Why Do I Never

Why am I never doing
what I'm supposed
to be doing?
I could be writing a poem –
should be writing a poem.
This better not become a poem
because then I'd be doing
what I'm supposed to be doing
and I'd stop.

Friendship for a Season

We lay all night on the cold grass
under sharp stars
and talked,
and as we talked
discovered how different
we really were.

This was the closest we had ever been
and the start
of our friendship's unravelling.

Funny, really, how we both went
from that pin-bright moment
into such separate lives.

Sometimes I'm sad
I could not love you.
But both of us have
that night –
that wide open talk,
those stars.

Sometimes I Wonder

if the people who educated me so well
stole a capacity for believing,

left me grieving the parts I was
told I had to lose.

I was too weird, too scatty, too confused
by the need to draw an A4-sized grid

and fit the figures neatly into it.
I'd rather let a daydream

comfortably defeat me than
grapple with a straight-line graph.

I learned, in the end,
as all good girls must do.

But I still wonder, sometimes,
how many poems

were lost to the strictures of
assessment objectives and analytical paragraphs,

how many drawings were defeated
by the need to solve a simultaneous equation –

an intellectual operation I managed simultaneously to
achieve and forget, the knack of it slipping

promptly from my head the moment I left the last exam.
I'm grateful to those people – please don't get me wrong –

many of them cared, and most of them tried to –

but I wonder if there's maybe irrecoverable treasure
that their didactic scales weighed as trash
to cast away.

I wonder if I do the same thing
to the minds I measure every day.

The Greenfinch
in the Garden

I was five the day I first discovered death.
A cat-got songbird on the lawn, frail, prone,
some final beauty to a mangled chest
that had been crushed mid-flight, a life undone;
I found a counting in my numbered breaths.

I carried the body about with me,
smoothing short feathers on the perfect head,
alive with a new-born empathy –
and then Dad saw us. *Wash your hands*, he said.
Instead I made a grave by the chestnut tree.

Once burial was done, I fled to my room,
sat cross-legged by the boarded fireplace
and one by one imagined every future tomb,
each person I loved in a cold, tight space,
their eyes limed over into sightless stones.

I stayed, there stuck in this enormity,
until, again, Dad came along, saw tears
and sat to share the carpet, growing kindly.
He listened as I gabbled out my fears –
why live at all when death's a certainty?

He did not laugh, or speak of God Above.
Instead he put a huge arm round my shoulders
and silently reminded me of love.
Then he said, *Why live? Well, for each other.*
Besides, we've all got so much left to prove.

Poem for an
Unheard Child

Her mother has a sadness in the bones and brain.
Family rush round and make food, but
nothing is the same.

In school she is cruel, and we sit in a stuffy classroom
as I try to make a space into which she can speak.

Perhaps we'll have better luck next week.

Cley Beach

for Dad

We spotted a seal pup, pretty in the pink-tinged sea of a
watercolour sunset, letting itself be rolled into shore, and
    laughed

then saw the mother fresh dead, lilted slightly by high tide's edge.

The pup was gone now and, though we watched through
    stretched minutes,
saw no dot of head in blackened water, so walked on,

shrunk by the day's-end gloom –

felt the pebbles disrupted by softness, tried not to tread on the
    corpses of starfish,
and still the night was beautiful. We held hands briefly, father
    and daughter,

then – accepting we could no longer see properly – drove home,
deciding what to have for supper.

The Dream

Someone has died in the dream.
I don't know who it is,
except that I had loved them.
I wander through a crowded room,
eyes roving over faces still as calm water,
until I find I cannot see my father.

I look no further for my father,
knowing I could wake from this dream,
but still the calm faces – blank as clear water –
are crowding in, and it is
clear they expect me to address the room.
I have nothing to say to them.

I have everything to say to them,
yet the words are lost with my father.
The man who leaves books in every room
of the house is wordless in this dream,
so even though I know this is
not real, my voiceless throat chokes as with water,

and the people staring seem to flow as water:
over the floor and up my static body I see them
flow, formless and forceful as a tide is
when it sweeps up the beach.
And though my father
stands on the beach at the edge of this dream,
and he is beckoning me out of that room,

the people-sea, now up to my torso, leaves me no room
to go to him: my knees buckle under the seething human-water;
my hands reach for his, where real seas lap the pebbled shore
    in his calm dream.
I shout for help, I scream, but he has turned to watch two seals
    and sing to them –
my far-away, warm, living father –
and his sea's breeze is cool, and my room's stuffy air is

hot, hot with the condensing sweat of the flowed flesh I'm
    sinking into. All is
slipped away, as I close my eyes on the room
with its liquidised faces and no father,
and imagine myself unstuck, beside him on pebbled beach
    before blue water.
Yet still a tugging current of hands pulls me to return my
    mind to them,
in this blank, drenched place which will, one day, be more
    than dream.

Now their sea crushes me; savage bodies of the water
rush me away from my father, back in thought and all to them.
In that inevitable dream. In that crowded room.

In Crovie

I am restless by the waves.
The gulls gust between tetchy and placid.

Sky loops over me like I'm in the basket
of a massive blue balloon.

The tide trails out,
dragged by a gently tyrannous moon.

The people walk along the beach and gaze
at the dual emptiness of sea and sky,

which holds within its ever-stretching width
uncounted lives: the fishes and the birds,

the slow instinctual pulsings of anemones,
the unseen scuttles of weed-homed crabs.

I breathe in fresh-flung salt and the sticky smell
of half-rotten seaweed. I try to remember

that I am a creature too, subject also to the
slow turning of things. I wish I had gills

and a shell, so I could swim and float and wallow,
waking from sleep in far-flung seas – always home.

Holkham Beach

Dig your fingers into sand.
Feel it pucker, yielding
under touch.

Feel the moisture held
an inch beneath
the sun-crunched surface.

Push down with your feet now.
Entomb them.
Let them be held
by the crumpled crumbs of aeons.

Hold yourself here,
in this space,
this place,
this breath.

What Remains

There is a strength in being loved
which never leaves, but sits
deep in the body,
waiting to be needed;

there is a happiness in loving back
which lets the strength sing
and makes ironing work shirts
much less annoying;

because we know that, at the end,
love is taken with us into the ground
where it grows trees,

or else we throw it up
in handfuls of ashes
for the wind to sow out widely
whipping into a huge blue sky
over a flat grey sea.

Dig

In our trench I found a body,
foetal in a fifteen-hundred-year-old rubbish tip.

The cemetery was down the hill,
the corpses there stretched proud and long,
coins about their ankles
and bangles round the flaking wrists.

It took four days to brush him from the ground –
thin hips suggested gender;
with each emerging bone I knew him better
as, knelt under voices discussing
the punitive nature of this burial,
I fought the boredom of repetition
with a will not to snap or splinter.

My man had oyster shells for coins;
the discolouration of rotted rope
prettied the structure of his once-tied hands;
and through long August hours it seemed the head was missing.

Eventually I turned it up, feeling rude, as
I stroked away the soil from his skull,
found its curve cut,

my careful finger tracing the fissure
from which the flow had
stopped

Lady Macbeth

went mad with no preamble.
The blood was gone, but then
it stained deep into skin.

The babe was lost
so she made a king,
and when she felt him slipping
all sense was sloughed away.

Perhaps if she'd had a career
she would have been OK.

Bombay Bike Ride

A 4 a.m. wrench out of bed,
then caffeine as we congregate.
Now pick a bike and enter lingered night,
a muffled street peopled by sleepers,

then the bay – electric lights
above a stirred sea.
Young men walk to work
holding hands, bleary and amused
to see tourists up so early. Follow

the curve of shore to a fishing port
awake already with women setting stalls,
men gathered to boats. One
sees me yawn and agrees with a nod
and half a smile. A

dog runs with us, barking joy
when she sees the guide, a
daily companion for her
with his fleets of speeding strangers.

Now more markets:
meat with a blood-rinsed floor, then

flowers dripped in strings down
fragrant alleys, a smell soured
by tales of terrorists; a bomb hidden here
in a motorbike last year. Mumbai

is coming out to join us now,
the city waking up –
children perched in front of dads on mopeds,
parcelled into uniform for school.
Chickens, goats and ox-carts
in amongst the traffic;

'Watch out!' I shout as
one lurches past us. 'Watch out!' I am
mimicked by a giggling school-boy bunch.

Suddenly a temple loud with devotees
to Mumba Devi 'Mother Goddess'. Some
pray another way, feeding the cows. We
join them and are licked by strong
demanding tongues. Soon

we are home, exhausted, still excited,
taking moments to unplug from the streets,
stood bemused and dirty
in the cool AC of a hotel lobby, unwilling
yet unable to prevent the past three hours
from slipping into memory.

Urban Hunting

City eagles wheel above us
watch for vermin

indifferent beauty
on black wings
they live quietly

to my eyes
a bird of prey
is something to be noticed

here there are
too many stories

we are clouded into the streets
and into ourselves

we miss the birds
miss their high sight

and silence.

On Disobedience

Jimmy thinks neglect is violence.
I am not so sure.
Seb thinks that we always need
the letter of the law.

Jim sucks Seb's words down
with a long slug of beer,
leans back, runs a hand
through his rumpled blond hair.

At the neck, passion precipitates
to drip and glisten on skin.
The plaid shirt bristles in creased red ripples:
his utterance now shall begin.

I snatch and hold breath
as he draws one in.
His voice leans along
the nasal angles of Dublin.

The bar smells of spilled lager
and manic fatigue.
Sweat sticks in the carpet.
I want to leave.

Seb's smaller than Jim,
slighter, and curled round his pint.
He grips the grey ends of his sleeves,
head bobbing to the cadence of his point.

I don't care any more what the arguments are.
Probably I should. I know that here
any idea I have will be
manfully withstood.

Now this tension between them is
clamping into fists –
it wants to throw up into punches.

And so I lean forward as conciliator,
the girl in the middle, to
calm, flatter, de-escalate, deflate.

Soon the three of us are laughing,
and I am silently irate.

Sonnet for Johnny

Remembering the time we met, six years
ago, I see your face so clearly; blue
eyes, sweet smile, quick laugh – I felt I knew you
instantly, so fast our friendship grew. Here
you were, willing to listen and share fears;
we talked a post-work drink away like two
flat-capped old men; our shared hours quickly flew,
but then you tried to fuck me. I felt smeared,
dirty. Sure it must have been my fault,
I gave a blow-job to keep you happy.
Again I taste your semen in my mouth
and gag with anger. Since then I've fought
the thing inside that seeks only to please.
You're the one who wasn't good enough, not me.

On Those Cold
December Evenings

Well you can just fuck off!
you say as I get 94
for 'indicate' across a triple word score.

I cackle,
you sniff;

always we act our way through:
bad poker faces,
elaborate sighs;

strategic trips to the cupboard
for more whisky
give delicious seconds
for savouring whether
the opposing party
has irritable vowel syndrome
or the makings
of a seven-letter *triumph.*

Our rules have been essentially the same
since you made my phone say
'bint' instead of 'silent'
when we were thirteen:
an abundance of well-meaning piss-taking
has made us siblings
something neither of our mothers
can quite understand.

I am sat by the window;
That is a ridiculous dog.
you laugh and come to look.
Half peke, half poodle? we speculate.

You linger,
we hug.
A quiet kind of love.

Seven and out.

Evening Song

We are safe in this sadness tonight,
for it is the kind kind, contained:
a thing for sharing;

it is Nina Simone's gently throbbed contralto,
crying of wrongs but finding the joy in today too,
noting out a hope for a thousand happier daughters;

it is my friend David lying in his last bed making
jokes about Snickers bars, and us
making jokes about Snickers bars back and
David saying *See you at choir next week*
and me meeting his eyes with
'Course I will.

It is an unspoken certainty
that each of us is saving tears up
to spare the others;

it is the making of this poem
and the giving of it to you;

it is the arms that hug
and the tongues that make randomness less terrifying.

We are rescued from silence tonight
because we have made its contemplation
a thing for sharing;
it has been contained as
the kind kind of sadness.

We are safe.

A Song for the Solstice

It is dark in the mornings now.
We snuggle into duvets
as the snooze button burbles.

In the evenings
we drink and eat and laugh
and long for spring.

How strange of us
to celebrate new life
when the leaves on the trees
are dying.

How strange of us.
How glorious.
How human.

Home

for Christmas

All of these small, significant things:
a nod as he plops down a tea in that certain mug –
someone leaving a room
soon after the mention of a marriage –
the old-lick smell of an ancient cat, its growl
as the warm knee shifts.

All of these small, significant things:
a sharpened pencil scratching as it sketches –
the gift of exactly the right book –
and a house that makes familiar noises in the night.

All of these small, significant things:
the sticky smell of a moulting pine tree –
the sight of it lit and baubled, perched full of
painted wooden birds –
the way presents seem to breed beneath it
as December ages.

And all of these small, significant things
gather pace, galloping into the day itself:
stockings filled with socks and pants,
chocolate oranges and trashy magazines –
that hideous Santa-hatted green toy lizard
which is always contrived to appear somewhere,
staring tattily from worn-out googly eyes –

breakfast, with Buck's Fizz, maybe, and pain au choc –
carols low on the radio and lazy table talk –
then perhaps a walk –
and always the annual argument between cooks, where
someone is told to *bugger off!* –
more bubbles diffuse tension to laughter –
sizzling smells drift between rooms, and Grandma sits
sipping in state until

LUNCH –
a badminton rally of careful compliments
and chomping:
the capon, the pigs in blankets, the bolly-wallies, bread sauce,
    gravy,
the carrots and peas and roasties and parsnips and sprouts,
the braised red cabbage –
each item in its established receptacle, circuiting round
the resplendent, candle-lit table –
the special silver cutlery, reserved only for
days such as this, when someone can be bothered
to do all that washing up –
the wine in special cups, a different one for each of us –
the crackers and hats and gloriously awful jokes –

the weighted, content silence as everybody eats.

The pause for talk and water which precedes
ROUND TWO:
a pudding on fire, a cheer –
a cut-glass bowl of lethal brandy butter, spooned out
in glinting chunks to melt into its steaming, fruity bed –
washed down with sips of sunset-golden Tokay –
Can anybody manage a bite of cheese?
Perhaps it can wait for later, with the cake…

Now elders recline upon sofas, whilst
the young distribute presents:
each person's loot delivered to the
floor around their chosen seat.

All of these small, significant things have been
strung together into slowly evolving ritual for
seven decades and at least five houses now:
the set and characters change over time, but
the essence remains unchanged.

Each year we make something beautiful,
twining the old in with new:
as one branch tires and withers,
a new twig will spring from our roots.

The Scan

for Maudie, before I knew her name

News of new life
in a grey spring –
grainy image
on a screen.
Heart beating.
Tiny fighting bean.

In the Spiky Days
of Spring

This bed is so big
it might swallow a sleeper.

I am loved and yet
I wake in the night.

Nothing is neat here.

Thoughts turn to prickles
under skin.

I scuttle in and out of dreams.

When should I switch to the summer duvet?
I feel so lost I could almost pray.

Doggerel Days

The breath comes in
the breath goes out
the headlines roll along:

some people shot
some others drowned
a pop star sang a song.

Some words are said
some words are swallowed
others written down:

inside my head
they're beautiful
and possibly profound.

I want to rest
I need to rest
I've got to go to sleep:

these doggerel days
are sprawling
and the rhymes
are on repeat.

Internet Litany

Be interesting be funny be pretty be nice
be cool be fit be rich be right be his be hers
be theirs be in touch how touching
are we touching watch out are they watching
were you watching did you like it how'd you
like it like this be like this be like them
be like us we're better than them be better than them
be humble be grateful be true to yourself
be kind be caring who cares he cares she cares
we care this is grammar just a lush linguistic
love affair are you in love do you know what love is
i love you love her love him loving isn't easy
in a hundred and forty characters man it's easy
to sound sleazy when you only wanna tell the world
what's in your heart and maybe get it trending
what's trending who's trending are we trending
we wanna be on trend coz you can't depend
on last season's clothes and have you seen
game of thrones it's so great everybody dies
ned dies and rob dies and catelyn dies and the wife
dies and the baby in her womb dies and the little girl
dies inside her own mind and isn't it amazing and i

47

wonder what'll happen in the ending i'm guessing
everybody dies except jon can't die because he's
such a great guy and watching this stuff is not
a waste of time it's quality time it's me time it's us time
when we discuss it why else would you make your visit
but it's so great to see you how are you are you ok
what's new what's the news with you that's
old news be the new you that's so true really be real
be careful be bewitched by this be loved be in love
be sued be screwed screw you and your mamma too your
mum your mum's face your mum's mum's face that's just
your grandma's face you know what i mean if you
know what i mean do you know what i mean i know
you know what i mean really do you know what i mean
you are pretty mean you're a mean girl you're a bitch
don't gender this narrative so fucking comparative
what a troll you're on a sick fucking roll don't
fuck with me sean not you who's you do i mean
robin no sean fuck what face are you wearing why
with the hanging and the slitting and the drinking and
all those good men dying just a few good men again
not again once again where are the bloody women
even in fiction what's the story morning glory you're so funny
please subscribe subscribe subscribe

your video begins in 0.02, 0.01, 0.00
buffering buffering buffering

Goggle Box

I am sitting on a sofa
watching someone else
sitting on a sofa
watching a news anchor
sitting at a desk
watching a geek
sitting at a computer
watching the new
Star Wars trailer

and it occurs to me
that I could never explain this

to my granny.

Ready or Not

You've come round at the end of another grey day,
full of winter lingering, my flat a heated beacon in the dark.

Let's drip conversation deep into the plum-ripe evening:
pour me another whisky, darling,
reheat the cauliflower cheese,
grill some bacon to go with it and feel the fat spit –

kiss me by the radiator, fuck me on the bed –
let's feel our bodies breathe.

You see,

I'm tired of squinting for ill omens at the edges of Thursday
    afternoons
I'm tired of predictable stories and blandly pretty tunes
I'm tired of the desire for job security
I'm tired of Tories and spreadsheets and the mild dangers of
    crossing streets
I'm tired of finishing things and starting things
I'm tired of metre and rhythm and rhyme –
I'm tired of the pleasure of not measuring time

I'm tired of the fear.
I'm tired of not trying because of the fear
I'm tired of fearing the fear
I'm tired of fearing the failure which might follow the shedding
   of the fear

and I'm tired of searching for an ultimate truth
beyond the scientific certainty

that we are the children of a blasted star –
begun in timeless exodus of dust,
then mated down a billion generations;
this moment's answer to an equation
ever-evolving, a morphing thing of
sinew, thought and carbon,
two miniscule links in a chain,

and though your hand will one day wither,
for now it's here, fastened to mine.
Is it worth waiting for any greater sign?

Take me away to the sea, darling,
take me away to the shore;
it is not necessary, yet,
to be sure that we are sure.

After Winter

We've hauled through grey mornings
of days before spring.

Weeks slugged on,
clouds constantly gathering.

Green spears of daffodils
poked from the ground,
but in March snow came,
leaving London pristine
for a morning.

When the thaw flowed,
the city was a
sprawl of threading rivers.

We stayed in the warmth
of each other's arms
until the weather caught up with us,
and we stepped outside into sunshine.

Now the magpie grabs an enormous twig, and
flies defiantly upwards
under its weight,
stating an aim to procreate. The cat

lies lazy in the shade, but
one ear twitches
at the sound the magpie made.

Morning relaxes into afternoon.
We really should get going soon.

For Xanthi

I brought you some daffodils
to celebrate spring,
and you had no vase,
so stood them to attention in the necks of bottles
marshalled as soldiers on the kitchen table,
sentinels against return of dark,
yellow Voltigeurs abloom,
stretched at victory
happy.

Clementine

Rounded in the palm,
pierced by a probing thumb.
Tiny, fragrant sun.

Composer

You sit in the window's light and
summon music from air, silently.

Three fingers of your right hand flick the beat out.
Your tunes scoot away, unheard by me.

You were still in the softness of that oncoming sunset.
I wonder where your music went.

In the Early Morning

I sail my hand across
the flat white silence of a sheet
to cradle your neck,
feel the body smiling under skin.
Here, lips and limbs
do all the talking.

What's a Trap?

Boxes can be houses or cages and
I don't know which this is so now I sit
to read, write, watch, sleep, think and dream of you –
or not of you, depending on my mood.

Are you in a cage now or a house? Are
your hopes resting smug on struts or are they
crunched into the cellar, mouldering down?
Boxes can be houses or cages and

who can tell where the blank place ends and the
feeling has seeped into brick and carpet?
Why do we like old houses, anyway,
with their untold histories of death in

every room? Better perhaps to go new-
build. Firm foundations under open sky.

Restoration Works

The deeper I wander into the house of you
the more I notice cracks
in your foundations
as you see weeds that weaken mine.

And yet.
We put aside
the surveyor's questions
to build a wall and roof above us,
brick on brick and slate on slate.

We hope that hope
will hold it up.

You Really Should
End this Thing

Here it is again, the fear of falling:
I catch myself half-tumbled from our bed.
Something in the deep of me is stalling.

As you hold me, words resist my calling;
I reach out – they tumble from my head.
Here it is again, the fear of falling.

When your charms are at their most enthralling,
it is so tempting merely to be led –
but something in the deep of me is stalling.

Your hands are skilled – they leave me wet and sprawling;
but they cannot build up walls against this dread:
it gushes through again, the fear of falling.

The thought of losing you is just appalling:
it's hard to wish another in your stead.
But something in the deep of me is stalling.

I cannot help but wonder why I'm crawling
up and up when half my mind has fled.
Then when I back away it feels like falling.
Something in the deep of me is stalling.

A Capital Story

for Stephen

A London summer night between thunderstorms
and the bus is diverted by a
pair of fluorescent policemen
rooted in the Walworth Road.

We slide down a side street and roll half a mile
before the driver lets me off –
Only official stops allowed –
and so here I am in the de-peopled Heygate Estate,
brutalist blocks marked out for the bulldozer.

The thunder seems closer.

Knowing I'm near home,
but not quite how to reach it,
I turn into a pub, the type where every drinker's white
and sour stains stick feet to carpet,
to ask the way to Fielding Street.

Are you all right walking home this late at night, love?
I can call you a taxi...
I say, *Thanks, I'm fine*, and start to leave when,
I'd walk you home myself if I wasn't so fucked
slurs a bar-stool charlie.
You better watch out for all them darkies.

Minutes later I've come out by the market,
like the sober one said I would, and the thick air shifts melody.
I register Bob Marley, then realise it's Christian reggae:
No, Jesus, no cry
No, Jesus no cry
Do you remember
When we used to sing...
Half the street is humming, from those same policemen
to the junkies outside the 24-hour shop.

Round the corner, home,

kids run down our street,
playing catch with a half-burst grapefruit.

The tall one laughs and lobs –
glass breaks.
They shriek
and run.

Sweeping the shards up,
I tip them into the centre of an old newspaper
and wrap, holding today in my hands.

The sharp sugar juice on the windowsill,
the singing and the roadblocks,
the blokes drinking lager,
the jobsworth driver,
the patient coppers,

the need for rain.

Central Line Sonnet

A mouse minus tail skirts a Lucozade bottle
at the bottom of an underground railway tunnel.
I climb on the train above his scuttling,
sit across from a boy
whose lit eyes match sun-swept hair.
Some mutually enquiring glances later
he leaves at Liverpool Street, and I wish I'd
had the courage to scribble my number
on a ripped-off corner of the evening paper
to hand him with my name and an enigmatic smile.
I while away the rest of my journey wondering
how he might have replied, had I summoned the
chutzpah in time. But that mouse and I, we both
waited too long, bounded by unseen lines.

After

Death of a Salesman

The ending hit me like a – well, you get the idea.
Not wanting to talk, I peeled off from the others to
    walk myself home,
shaking with unaskable questions.

I stood a long time on Charing Cross Bridge,
listening to a busker play Spanish guitar,
letting London seep into my confusion,
letting the fierce, smashed-up life of it enter as a torrent of
reflection from the river, transformed from the day's
muddy brown into a darkling, shimmered, glittering thing.

I stood a long time, and the busker saw,
nodding to include me at the height of a phrase,
so that I felt a part of this moment's furniture,
and leant less tensely on the railing, committing to
my role now, felt the susurrations of my city
as the drifted speech of walkers lulled and swelled,
counterpointed by the sloshing, moon-guided Thames,

the self-confidence of Big Ben's knells,
by the busker's acoustic arpeggios.

Both of us watched the people go past:

the mother who stopped for a minute to listen,
her baby's legs kicking appreciatively;

the father who led his son forward by the hand,
and coaxed him to offer a glinting pound;

the city boy, suited and fully plugged in,
who marched to the beat of his AirPods;

the family posing for photos close by,
who jostled and twitched up their grins.

The music wound out from that upright old man,
twining in intricate lines,

and under us all, the glistening Thames,
billowing, ancient and mindless,
its tidal cacophony coursing a melody:
fast and yet fastening – timeless.

Too Long in London

Take me to the lonely places,
where there's no Deliveroo.
Take me to the wild spaces,
where the wolves can come for you.
Cut the WiFi, chuck the phone:
let us really be alone.

Choir Away Weekend

Out of London finally, the old
slam-door train trundling us through
a huge East Anglian sunset.

Met by friends in Saxmundham and then
on, car-crowded, surrounded by smells
of fidgeting dog and dusty July day,
on until road becomes track
and then runs out
beside the cliff-cut sea.

Dinner under the last of the day's light,
then suddenly the stars,
at first only the obvious ones, before
further layers are called through by adjusted focus,
until enmeshed constellations blaze away,
with living fire, or mere light's memory – we can't tell.

Inside again we sing,
Draw on, sweet night,
tensions sweeping out of us as music

when notes that have faltered
focus and come out right, to
slink above and under each other
in a silvered flow, so that
for those few togethered seconds
we are something more than we were,
a sort of whole, until a final cadence
brings us back to separate breath
and silence.

SOMEWHERE

Somewhere is the quiet we seek.
Somewhere in this dark.

Sometime is the time when things
are right. Some time, some night.

I'm not sure who you are,
or where you are, but hopefully
sometime, somewhere,
you will appear.

When you do, I hope we both
have the right words.

Sometimes I worry that we may
have met and parted,
with the right words trailing
between us, half-mumbled.

Hopefully somewhere, some time,
you will read this and smile;
knowing I was wrong,
knowing we said the right words,
knowing we made something
TRUE.

SOMETIME

BACH ON THE BRAIN:
A prelude to the prelude in C major...

When I try the tune I always falter after several bars I
cannot find a perfect pace I can't get past this certain place it's
really rather stupid as I've played this piece a thousand times but
when the printed notes are gone I always seem to get it wrong my

fingers try their best but still I cannot quite impress upon them
how the notes must go they just keep playing the beginning they're on
loop and they won't slow to give my brain the time to work it out it
gets me so frustrated when they run away from rightness it's truth

slipping out of sight and beauty waking in the night in panic
looking for some comfort in the obvious but none is found it's
never quite that silvered sound you've heard in Gould's recording when the
met - ro - nom - ic beat contains a glinting stream of stories and if

you can listen carefully you'll hear that he is softly singing
following his fingers with a quiet yearning humming but I
didn't mean to put that in my thoughts are drifting with this poem
it's not sure what it is saying maybe it is saying nothing

why does everything we make get burdened with such weighty meaning
even spoons and pillow-cases carry memory within them
Mum and Dad and Sunday tea and visitors and ironing I'm
dipping into childhood now but not insightfully just writing

on and on to let it out although I'm not sure what needs letting:
how to go to work tomorrow? How to face ultimate ending
how to find a key I can play through my days in without spending
all my nights in sleepless restless fear with my brain upending

every worry I have had in childhood and adolescence -
never mind I can't defeat my mind I'll just have to live in it
even worst scenarios will surely end up having merit
and all fugues must finish sometime on an interrupted cadence

Meltdown

If you feel overwhelmed by all the tasks you have to do, just make a manageable list and tick them off as you go.

I don't think I ever really was depressed -

BEGIN AT THE CHIN

① PAY more **OVERLOADED** (lazy) ② **FOLD THE LAUNDRY**

(a) THE ... to the point a safety

catch inside my mind somehow **SLIPPED**. (couldn't be bothered)

Wade in the **WATER**, wa-a-ade in the water, children,

It's already over-due, you know. **BILL** and also, check when...

FLIPPED ← (BRAIN) IMPLODED

and I ... plenty bonny **BAIRNS** as well — that's our wish

I screamed squashed sorrow from my

Remember that **GUTS** in Mum's kitchen,

spewed rage which had grown too strong for

CONTAINING...

Once I reached that place, I could no longer

keep the **pain in**

③ **PACK BAG** my life was a pus-filled

(a) **FOR WORK** ... **ZIT** —

and I was squeezing

before you go to sleep No more!" Macbeth hath murdered sleep.

tonight, little baby, don't you cry — Mama's gonna sing

gonna buy you a Mocking bird. Is that right?

Oh no — you didn't follow? Please **TRY HARDER** tomorrow.

Once again, nothing has been accomplished. Disappointing work.

Stop your infantile whining. Everyone else can manage to pay their bills on time: you could too, if you just got on with it.

Why is you keep the pain in are you be packing your bag? Youtubing Dolly Parton when you should be...

You're clearly not trying hard enough.

You are a little baby. It's pathetic.

It doesn't matter.

continue

Decisions

I heard Jarvis Cocker say on the radio once
that the day never starts until he's
put his glasses on. He enjoys this decision
to begin action each morning,
to throw off the fug of sleep at a
moment of his own choosing.

For me, some days, this is one
decision too many, one more amidst
a life made up of them:
left or right,
her or him,
Tube or bus,
sit or stay standing.

Some days I refuse
to make that first decision – refuse
to see anything beyond my bedroom.
This, in itself, is a decision:
a decision not to decide today.

I suppose that is how people arrive at suicide,
when one more decision
precludes all those to come;
one little movement and the
making of days will be done;
no more left or right,
no more her or him,
no more Tube or bus,
no more sitting or standing,
just one more little movement,
then a blank –
a soft absence of sight;
a nothing.

Just as morning's still revolving
before we choose to see it,
so the hours will be lived in when we're gone:
it can be no release from pain
merely to pass it on.

Late Diagnosis

for Mum, who knew what to do

Mum is taking me to see a psychiatrist.
I think she's frightened.
That makes two of us. The other night
I screamed about –
I don't remember what.
My whole body shook,
and my throat hurt,
and I cried on the terracotta tiles
of her kitchen floor.
She looked down at me,
and her face was like that of a cat
in a tree being dive-bombed by crows.

She doesn't know about the train
on Platform B where I nearly –
well. I know. And so I doubly know
that she is right to take me here.
Car crunches over long gravel drive:
we've arrived. Outside, people
walk quietly over immaculate grass in pairs.

I'm scared. I hug Mum.
Her curly hair pillows under my chin.
Squeeze. Let go. I walk in. Remind
myself I won't be staying. Wait amidst
a controlled, blue-carpeted hush.

My name is called. I climb up too many
stairs. Turn. Walk. Knock.
The doctor has steady, weighing eyes
behind reassuring steel-framed glasses.
I have put my *I'm fine* face on and
manage to shake hands, greet him cordially.
He gestures to a squashy chair.
Beside it a box of tissues stands ready.
I need them. My *fine* face slips off within
ten minutes, as I tell him about all
the sounds I can't block out, and how
everyone always expects excellence,

but my mind, which can run so fast and
silvered, so funny and so kind, rebels.
Every time. I tell him how the antidepressants
aren't working and how
they are making me sleep all day, and how
I can't stop crying, and how
dirty dishes mound up wherever I am,
unseen, like fucking snipers waiting to
get me. I tell him about the
diagnoses of Depression and Anxiety, about the
bricks of disappointment I've walled up
between myself and my friends,

myself and my myself, myself and my family. About the
forgotten birthdays and unsent thank-you cards and failed
relationships and crumpled clothes and mess. About the
years of therapy trying to accept myself –
but how can I accept me
when I continue to be so
thoughtless, so useless, so lazy?
I tell him about Platform B.
About how I don't want to die,
but I can't stay nothinged here much longer either.
At the end of an hour, he tells me, gently,
that he thinks I have ADHD.

I stop. Shock. *But,* I say, *but I'm not a hyper little boy.*
His smile is not mocking.
A little boy? No. But hyper? Look at your hands.
I do. The fingers twist around,
incessant. They stop. *And your foot.* I look.
It's jiggling. It freezes. *Oh. That counts?*
The patient smile again. *It does.*
He doesn't make a diagnosis right away. Says I
have forms to fill in, and so do my friends and
family. And that I should do some reading.
See if what I learn makes sense for me,
then come back another day.

I walk out into sunshine and fresh air,
striding past the quiet strolling pairs,
up the winding gravel drive, out the curlicued front gate,
and down the pavement to a public park.
Swans swish along, children climb trees.

I sit on a bench. Breathe.
I ring Mum and tell her the news.
That it seems to make sense. That it's common
for girls, then women, to receive a late diagnosis,
because boys will be boys but
girls – well girls must be good. I'm shaking again.
I was trying hard. I was trying so hard all along.

It's Quiet in Here

I hadn't even known it was loud.
Hadn't realised my brain was a radio
flicking between stations, or –
more often than not – tuned to two/three/
four at once – a constant
current swirling tunes and thoughts and
static – metaphors, emotions – mixed
like a dozen DJs' messy ends-of-nights
stretched out over days,
over decades, over every moment lived in – an
unceasing lifetime of

NOISE.

And now, an hour after swallowing this pill,
dead on schedule,
the channels have merged into one,
and it is filled with

silence.

I can choose which thought to follow next.

First, I tidy my bedroom. All of it.
Then I sit down on the clean, empty carpet.
I listen to the quiet.

I weep.

Acceptance

Acceptance is a small, quiet room,
its ceiling the blue of a still, summer sky.
For years I thought the door was locked –
I was too scared even to try the

handle. The first few attempts, it
jammed. I'd jiggle it up and down.
When I finally forced it open,
walls were waves, eager to drown.

So I ran – but oiled the hinges,
occasionally peeking round.
Later, I'd creep in and listen to that ocean groaning loud,

until slowly, so slowly, the hurricane
eased to a breeze:
the storm clouds gave way to horizon,
and my body began to unfreeze.

Pandemic Diary

March–December 2020

The country's been put into a lockdown,
to flatten the curve of Covid-19.
Right now, the virus is out of control,
so doctors urge us all to stay inside.
I cuddle up with Netflix and the cat,
hoping wise heads prevail in Government.

There's obvious chaos in Government:
they left it too late to start a lockdown.
Thousands – we think – now have Covid-19.
Without mass testing, how can we control
this *thing*, this mundane killer spread inside
our homes, our hospitals? I hug the cat.

I get a meaningful glare from the cat.
She needs some personal space. Government
allows one walk per day during lockdown:
a slump around the park. Covid-19
could be lurking on each bench. Must control
this anxiety. I hurry inside.

There's nothing much to do now, stuck inside.
I make a cardboard racecourse for the cat,
and watch endless briefings from Government.
They say we must stay patient with lockdown:
it will slow the spread of Covid-19,
and help us get things more under control.

My seeping isolation takes control.
I fear myself, and cannot stay inside.
Dear friends say, *Come to us!* I take the cat.
We think this is allowed: the Government
guidelines aren't too clear. We're still in lockdown –
together. We drink. *Curse Covid-19*.

The Prime Minister has Covid-19.
We are not sure who is now in control.
This flat feels very small when stuck inside.
A speeding car runs over my poor cat.
She dies. I fucking hate the Government.
Weeks become months. In and out of lockdown.

December: Lockdown Three. I catch Covid-19.
The man in control – who says *stay inside* –
hosts a fat-cats' Christmas party in Government.

Still Lockdown

I am so tired the corners of my
eyes are crying. Foetal in bed, arms wrapped
around heart-casing chest, I writhe over
why I can't cradle myself into rest.
This beat in limbs and brain won't halt for breath –
even sleep is rhythmic, little rest;
I have too much propriety to scream –
the thoughts abounding round are too obscene,
too beautiful to write or drop or hold.
Air pulses up from my lungs:
teeth clamp tongue in prison walls of gums.

Returning Song

Zoom choir was shit. I hated it:
the ache of familiar faces caught in a laptop,
seconds out of sync, each of us singing alone
to a muted screen.

But when summer came we were able to meet in a garden.
Spaced the obligatory six feet apart, we drank and spoke and
laughed and listened and sang – really sang, our voices
slightly husky, out of use, but still there, still willing
to twine and drop and soar – to weave a living story in the air.

We sang until the sunset stole our light.
The neighbours all came out to hear, and clapped
behind their fences. That scattered applause
was better than the roars of a rock-star crowd:
it welcomed the return of a pleasure shared.

Settled

for Pradyumna

When I said I loved you
and you said it too,
something settled.

Then, when I got sick, you stayed.
You brought me water
when I had forgotten I was thirsty.
I taught you how to proofread properly.

I began watching Arsenal.
You took a tentative interest in poetry.

Panic itched to run
because this –
well, this has never happened.

I grin like a kid every time you
recite from *Blackadder* as Robbie Coltrane
whilst making a cup of coffee.

We snuggle up together on the sofa.
The cat settles down on the rug
at our feet.

The curtains are closed,
the fairy lights twinkle.
Everything feels gathered in.
Your head rests on my arm.

Calm.

Finally This Feels Right

It feels like a curse to put into words
How deeply it is that I need you.
How strongly my viscera twists at the thought
That one day I might be without you.

You are the first person to see who I am
and gather me in so completely.
You share in my space and my mess and my shame
And sweep it aside, to complete me.

Hopefully Not an Elegy

If you read this in a future century,
I hope you are familiar with paper.
I hope you've learned its touches, smells
and looks, its dapples, feels and shades.
I hope you've felt a fountain pen's velveteen slink
and a biro's workaday scamper.

I hope you've found that horrifying, half-filled teenage diary
in a loft-shoved, dust-gritted cardboard box marked:
    'RANDOM STUFF'.
I hope you've skimmed through it, squelched right over with cringe,
and then held it carefully under a lighter, because on the internet
nothing can burn, and a thirteen-year-old's ill-judged crush, or
    momentary
irrational hatred of their sister, shouldn't be traced to them for ever.

I hope you have notebooks – many of them – jostling for space in
drawers and on bedside tables, silently asking to be scribbled in,
or opened to remind you what you thought of that play you saw
last year, or how kind your boyfriend was last September, or
how much you enjoyed the tide-fresh calamari you ate in
Andalucía on that sandy, sun-drenched July holiday.

I hope you have reading books – many of them – collected
since childhood and hauled though uncounted house moves.
I hope you've lingered your fingers on the edges of pages half-
read, impatient to flick your way through the story faster.
I hope you have a ceiling-high case full of books:

favourite books, with white-lined bent-back spines, peeling-off
covers – ineptly stuck back on with wonky tape – and years-old
post-it notes poking out to mark important places,
or yellowed, wavy pages where you dropped them in the bath,
and dried them out on the radiator later, unable to throw
something so precious away, no matter how damaged;

worthy books, on subjects which ought to interest you, bought
in solemn moments of intended self-improvement or bestowed by
well-meaning givers, which sit pristine for years,
slanting you unread, reproachful sidelong glances;

special books, given to mark Christmases, anniversaries, birthdays or
achievements, dated and inscribed with perfect messages
from brothers, sisters, parents, friends and lovers;

weird books, picked up at village fêtes and market stalls,
or in the whiffy basements of second-hand bookshops –
the sort with a silent, bespectacled owner and a resident cat,
which take up an entire elderly townhouse on an enigmatic
side street in Cromer, New Delhi or Versailles;

books you intended to give as gifts, but started perusing instead,
then couldn't give away because you folded down a corner, so
now it looked too read.

I hope you have books who become dear friends, so that a
    glimpse
of the title, as you plod past to fold laundry, jerks your
bored lips into a fond half-smile.

Dear Twenty-Second Century Reader,
I commend to you the joys of paper,
for once it is yours it stays yours:
to share, to squander or to treasure.

Acknowledgements

I owe a huge debt of gratitude to the first readers who read and responded to early drafts of the poems in this book. Your honest, insightful comments and kind words of support were invaluable. Thank you.

Will Dady	Simon Mundy
Tony Haynes	Jane Salvage
Stephen Irwin	Deborah Spring
Pradyumna Jairam	Charles Whalley
Ben Lund-Conlon	

A massive thank-you is also due to those who provided much-needed encouragement and feedback on individual poems:

Laura Graham	Theo Lester
Ashok Gupta	Hannah Lewis
James Henshaw	Maud Millar
Lisa Hirst	Debs Mullett
Rachel Irwin